Vampires in Mythology

Diane Bailey

rosen publishing's
rosen central

New York

Published in 2012 by The Rosen Publishing Group, Inc.
29 East 21st Street, New York, NY 10010

First Edition

Library of Congress Cataloging-in-Publication Data

Bailey, Diane.
Vampires in mythology / Diane Bailey.
    p. cm.—(Vampires)
Includes bibliographical references and index.
ISBN 978-1-4488-1227-1 (library binding)
ISBN 978-1-4488-2230-0 (pbk.)
ISBN 978-1-4488-2235-5 (6-pack)
1. Vampires. I. Title.
GR830.V3B33 2012
398'.45—dc22

                                                                2010018464

Manufactured in Malaysia

CPSIA Compliance Information: Batch #S11YA: For further information, contact Rosen Publishing, New York, New York, at 1-800-237-9932.

On the cover: The Hindu goddess Kali is a powerful goddess with the head of a demon and signifies time, change, and death. The evolution of her legend helped birth the idea of death-bringing monsters, including vampires.

CONTENTS

INTRODUCTION

AS vampires go, Count Dracula was doing pretty well. Sure, he lived alone, in a dank, creepy castle, with bats for company. But he was also wealthier and better looking, and had a lot more nifty powers than his ancestors. In fact, when Dracula appeared in Bram Stoker's novel in 1897, he barely resembled the vampires that had existed in mythology for thousands of years.

Today, vampires are everywhere in our culture. A vampire might be a mysterious high school student who all the girls like, a misunderstood loner with no social life, or a friendly character on the outside of a cereal box.

Many modern vampires are attractive and likable. But centuries ago, vampires were pretty gross creatures, unlikely to make anyone's "hottie" list. They were usually ugly, half-rotted corpses in serious need of a bath. Their breath was terrible—a vampire in Chinese culture could even kill with its obnoxious breath!

There will always be a debate between people who believe in the existence of vampires and those who do not. But one thing is clear. Even if vampires are not actual "real" creatures, the myth of vampires is very real. The belief in these creatures has influenced people's behavior for thousands of years.

Myths are stories that people have made up to help explain their world. For example, ancient cultures did not understand why the seasons changed or why volcanoes erupted. So they invented stories that explained these events.

From ancient times on up to the 1700s, vampires were more than just scary creatures. They served a real purpose in society, helping people to explain death, disease, and other evils. Did someone die mysteriously? Vampires must have gotten to him. Did the wheat crop fail? Was there an earthquake? Probably the vampires' fault. Even minor problems, like nightmares or headaches, might be blamed on vampires.

Vampires even brought people together. No matter what your differences with your parents or friends, you could agree on one thing: vampires were bad.

In early mythology, vampires were living creatures that terrorized people. Later, they gained even more power by being able to cross the line between living and dead. It turned out being "undead" was a convenient way to irritate the living without having to suffer the consequences. This ability to come back from the grave and move between worlds has given vampires a special place in mythology.

By the nineteenth century, the vampire's role was beginning to change. Science had cleared up a lot of the mysteries of death, so vampires became more the stuff of horror novels. And by the twentieth century, vampires came in all forms. Some were disgusting. Others were charming. We were as likely to love them as we were to hate them. We might feel sorry for them, or we might envy their special powers and place in the world. We might—if we were to be totally honest—even wish to be one.

UNWANTED VISITORS

WANTED: Dead or Alive. If only it were that easy! Vampires are neither dead nor alive. They're a little bit of both. As dead people who have returned to take possession of their earthly bodies, they are now "re-animated corpses." They are the undead.

FROM DEMONS TO DEAD MEN

In the earliest traditions, vampires weren't dead. They weren't even undead. Instead, they were very much alive. They were like cannibals, eating the flesh and blood of others. People thought they were demons or evil spirits. They weren't called vampires—that word didn't show up until the 1700s. These creatures were a sort of prototype for later vampires. These early models changed through the centuries, but one thing stayed the same: they preyed on people.

Blood was at the top of the vampires' "favorite foods" list. Early people believed that a person's life-force was contained in the blood, so it was the perfect

Vampire-like creatures would often feed on their victims while they were sleeping. In this 1781 painting *The Nightmare*, by Henry Fuseli, a woman is helpless to fend off her attackers.

energy drink. However, sometimes vampires sucked out a person's psychological or emotional energy. Psychic, or spiritual, vampires often hypnotized their victims to get them to cooperate. *Succubi* were female vampires, and their male counterparts were called *incubi*. They were angels who had been rejected from heaven and had turned into demons. They would sneak in at night and feed off people's energy.

Gradually the status of vampires changed. Instead of being evil demons, they became revenants. "Revenant" comes from a French word that means "return." These beings had returned from the dead and taken possession of their earthly bodies. In part, this change was due to the influence of Christianity, as it spread through medieval Europe. People believed that sinful souls did not go to heaven and were doomed to live in their earthly bodies as vampires.

Some cultures had two types of vampires—living and dead. In Romania, the *moroi* were living, while the *strigoi* were dead. (The *strigoi* were worse.)

Still another form for vampires to take was an "astral projection." Some people believed that people have two parts: their physical body and their spiritual soul. If the soul was angry or depressed, it might leave the body and turn into a vampire.

DEMEANOR

Whatever their state of mortality—living, dead, or somewhere in between—early vampires were not pleasant creatures. They were ugly and bloodthirsty. It was only much later, thanks to books and movies, that vampires discovered the wonders of shampoo and developed some social skills. Maybe they thought that they'd better clean up their acts if they were going to be famous!

Paul Barber writes in his book *Vampires, Burial, and Death*:

If a typical vampire of folklore, not fiction, were to come to your house this Halloween, you might open the door to encounter a plump Slavic fellow with long fingernails and a stubby beard, his mouth and left eye open, his face ruddy and swollen. He wears informal attire—in fact, a linen shroud—and he looks for all the world like a disheveled peasant. If you did not recognize him, it is because you expected—as would most people today—a tall, elegant gentleman in a black cloak. But that would be the vampire of fiction.

In ancient myths, vampire-like beings did not even always appear human. The Indian goddess Kali had four arms and wore a necklace made of skulls. The vampire-like *brahmaparusha* didn't have a body at all; it simply had a head and a trail of intestines. The *asasabonsam* of the Ashanti

In Indian mythology, the goddess Kali was associated with disease, death, destruction, and war. She was ugly and frightening, and her bloodthirsty nature was the subject of many gruesome stories.

tribe of Africa look basically like humans, but instead of feet, they have hooks. They live in trees and snag their prey from above. Then, they bite its thumb with teeth made of iron.

Modern vampires usually have fangs—the better to pierce their victims' skin and suck their blood. However, fangs became associated with vampires only in the 1900s. The *aswang* of the Philippines had a hollow tongue to sip through, but in most mythologies, vampires lacked such handy tools. And they didn't have any table manners at all. They simply ripped their victims apart to get their blood.

The Romany people (sometimes known as Gypsies) believed that vampires looked more or less normal, except for one thing, such as an arm that looked like an animal's or a missing finger. In Bulgaria, vampires had only one nostril, while in Mexico they had no skin on their skulls.

In some cultures, however, vampires looked identical to humans. They could blend in with regular people—making them even more scary.

POWERS AND WEAKNESSES

Being undead had its perks. Not only had vampires cheated death to move among the living, but now they didn't even have the problems regular humans had to deal with, like getting sick or injured. They could bring animals under their control and even had the ability to shape-shift into different animals, such as foxes, wolves, cats, or butterflies. Once in this other form, they assumed the abilities of these animals—such as keener eyesight or hearing. Vampires could even change into inanimate objects, like fog. In this form, they could escape their graves through small holes in the ground. Once they re-entered the world of the living, they could shift back into human form, making it easier for them to catch their victims off guard.

Count Dracula recoils from a crucifix in this movie made around 1960, starring actor Christopher Lee. Christian symbols and items were believed to hurt vampires.

However, vampires had limitations as well. One belief was that they could not enter a home without being invited. They could also be kept at bay with garlic or religious items such as crosses or holy water. They couldn't travel over water, and even though they came out at night, they were still tied to their graves for at least a few hours each day.

These weaknesses did not show up in all stories, however. Russian peasants believed that vampires roamed around in the daytime, keeping a noon-to-midnight schedule. Also, not all vampires had to be invited into the home. Some simply entered whenever they pleased. Others could reach a person through his or her dreams.

People in eastern Europe believed that after death, a person's soul hung around on earth for forty days, then tried to re-enter the body. Occasionally, this soul was successful. He became a vampire called a *strigoi*. Now that he had a new lease on deadly life, the *strigoi* had several years to grow into a human body and establish himself as part of the community.

POSSESSED PUMPKINS

Here's a reason not to let that Halloween pumpkin sit on the porch too long: after ten days, it might turn into a vampire. The Romany people of eastern Europe believed that certain fruits—such as pumpkins and watermelons—could turn into vampires if they weren't properly disposed of. Happily, pumpkin vampires weren't too dangerous. Although they might roll around and get in the way, they didn't have teeth and they didn't attack people. Plus, they could be destroyed easily; just put them in some boiling water.

He didn't need to return to his grave each night, and he laid off the blood and switched to regular food. With his diet no longer a problem, he could now mingle among the living, even getting married and having a family. However, immortality had its price. After several years of not getting any older, people might start to notice. Therefore, these undercover vampires had to stay on the move, never remaining in one place for too long.

THE VAMPIRE'S AGENDA

The main problem with being dead is that you're no longer alive, and vampires caught on to this right away. Being dead, they could not manufacture any blood or energy of their own, which left them only one option if they wanted to hang out with the living: they had to steal from people who were still alive. People who reported being visited by vampires described how the vampire would press on top of them, controlling them. The vampire would then take something from his or her victim. Whether it was blood or psychological energy, people believed that vampires needed this sustenance from the living in order to maintain themselves. In a Romanian village, one woman consistently baked better bread than her neighbors. The other women concluded she was a vampire who had sucked the very "goodness" out of their bread and used it for her own.

Why didn't vampires just get dead, like they were supposed to? Many people believed that vampires were people whose souls were not at rest. Often they were angry at the living for not doing the things necessary for them to pass on. As a result, vampires often returned first to their own family members, who had botched the job of sending the vampire to the next world. Sometimes they would just break furniture or throw objects around the house. However, they might physically attack their loved ones. They might also attack livestock or other animals and drink their blood. Some people believed that vampires were simply lonely and returned to have some company.

Whether they destroyed bread or drank blood, all vampires did one thing: disturbed the living. And whatever their reasons, they were pretty stubborn about it. The living did not want anything to do with them, but vampires refused to take the hint.

VAMPIRES AROUND THE WORLD

IT'S difficult to know where vampires first originated. Many scholars believe the word "vampire" came from the Slavic word *upir*, which first appeared in written texts in the eleventh century. By the late twelfth century, English scholars were writing about reported vampire activity. However, vampire stories were being whispered from one frightened person to the next long before that, and in places far away from Europe.

ORIGINS OF VAMPIRES

In many ancient mythologies, vampire-like beings were roaming the earth thousands of years ago. People didn't call them vampires then. They were not revenants who had returned from the dead to live in their former bodies. However, they were still preying on the living— eating flesh, sucking blood, killing innocent people, and generally making mischief.

People from Greece, Rome, Persia, and Mesopotamia all had stories about flesh-eating monsters or blood-sucking demons. Archaeologists have found pictures on pottery from ancient Persia that show such creatures in action. Where did these demons come from? According to the ancient Egyptians, they were brought over from another world, through witchcraft, and later became the first vampires. In the ancient Greek tale *The Odyssey*, Odysseus calls up shades (ghosts of the dead) by making a sacrifice of fresh blood. Some of these ancient stories may have been combined with later vampire folklore.

In 2008, archaeologists uncovered a grave in the Czech Republic. The grave dated back to the Bronze Age, approximately four thousand years ago. Archaeologists noticed that the skeleton had two stones on top of it. They believe the stones were placed there to pin the corpse down and keep it from escaping the grave. Similar archaeological evidence for keeping potential vampires in their graves— and of killing them again if that didn't work—has been found in graves around the world.

A brick is wedged into the mouth of a woman who died from the plague. Many people believed vampires caused disease and that this burial ritual would prevent someone from becoming a vampire after death.

The appearance and habits of early vampires differed from culture to culture. They might be solid or ghostly. They might feed on blood or energy. They might look human or they might be a mishmash of human,

KEEPING IT ON THE DOWN-LOW

In Armenia, on Mount Ararat, lived Dakhanavar, a territorial vampire who could not stand for anyone to count the number of valleys in the mountains. Whenever people passed through, he killed them by sucking their blood through their feet. One time, two travelers slept in opposite directions, with their feet hidden under each other's heads. This confused Dakhanavar. He declared that he had never seen a person with two heads, and no feet, in all the 366 valleys of the mountains. The travelers survived their journey, and from then on, people knew the number of valleys in the mountains.

animal, and monster. However, they shared the same goal: to steal the life force of a person.

THE SAME, BUT DIFFERENT

Civilization is often said to have begun in Mesopotamia, an area now known as the Middle East. People there believed in a type of spirit known as the *edimmu*. The *edimmu* did not have bodies but were ghost-like figures that would suck energy from people. Unlike the wispy *edimmu*, the *empusa* from Greece were sturdier: they had bodies to help them get around. The Greeks also believed in the *lamia*, a female vampire that was human on top

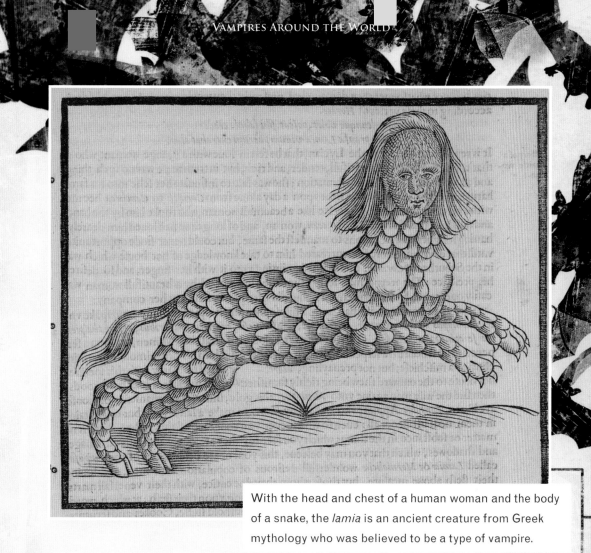

With the head and chest of a human woman and the body of a snake, the *lamia* is an ancient creature from Greek mythology who was believed to be a type of vampire.

and animal (usually a snake) on the bottom. In Viking folklore, the *draugre* were undead creatures whose bodies did not decay. They could also see into the future, control the weather, and change shape. In India, the *vetala* were demons who would use the bodies of dead people (not necessarily their own) to return and terrorize the living.

The Chinese believed that people had two souls—one good and one bad. After death, the bad soul sometimes stayed in a person's body. These beings were called *chiang-shih*. They had green or pink hair, and sharp teeth and talons. Sometimes they even glowed green. A body stiffens up after it dies. This is called rigor mortis. This condition made the *chiang-shih* hop around awkwardly.

African cultures had the *obayifo*, a witch who lived secretly in the community. At night, the witch could leave its body and take the form of a ball of light. It then attacked its victims and drank their blood. South and Central American countries also have their own versions of vampires. The *loogaroo* of Haiti, the *sukuyan* of Trinidad, and the *asema* of Surinam all closely resemble the witch-vampire of Africa. Historians believe these traditions were imported to the Americas by African slaves. The ancient Mayans worshipped a god named Camazotz, a half-human, half-bat monster that may have been based on vampire bats native to the region.

The role of the vampire differed from culture to culture, but there were also some similarities. For example, the Babylonians told a story of Lilitu, a female demon who drank the blood of babies. The Jewish religion may have used Lilitu as the basis for their tale of Lilith, the first wife of Adam (before Eve). Lilith and Adam had a falling out, and to seek revenge, she began to drink the blood of children. The *lamastu* from Mesopotamia also fed on babies, as did the Roman *strix*, which took the form of an owl. These myths all had one thing in common: the vampires attacked children. The stories were ways to explain miscarriages and infant deaths.

Many cultures had male vampires who attacked young women. They served as a warning to girls to listen to their parents and stay away from dashing young men who would only end up hurting them.

Aboriginal Australians feared the *yara-ma-yha-who*, a small, red man who lived in trees and waited for unsuspecting victims to fall asleep. He drank their blood, then swallowed them whole. After a bit, he vomited up his victim to see if the person was still alive. (He or she usually was.)

DON'T ANSWER THAT!

The Greeks believed that evil people, or ones who had been rejected from the church, were doomed to become *vrykolakas*—vicious vampires who killed both people and animals. There was an interesting defense against the vrykolakas: they would knock on doors and call out the names of the people who lived there. If the people answered, they were sure to die. However, the vrykolakas would call only once. If no one responded, they would move on. Therefore, it remains custom in some parts of Greece to wait until the second knock before answering the door.

Children learned about this vampire to warn them against wandering away from their villages.

INTO EUROPE

As people began to spread across the earth, so did their stories. Traders and travelers carried their stories to other places. You've probably played the game "telephone." One person whispers something to the person beside him or her. This person then repeats the sentence to the next person. After a few repetitions, the message is usually quite a bit different from the original. That's what happened with these stories. Certain details were added or

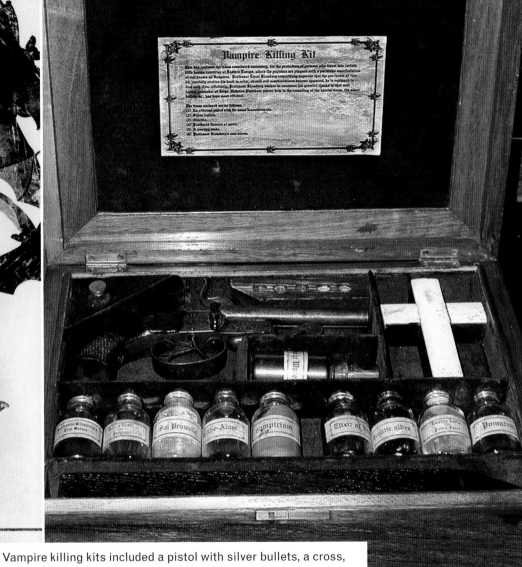

Vampire killing kits included a pistol with silver bullets, a cross, and various herbs to ward off vampires. Kits such as these were primarily sold in the 1800s and can be seen in museums today.

left out, depending on what the storyteller remembered or what he or she wanted to emphasize.

Much of our modern idea of vampires comes from eastern Europe, including Romania, Poland, Hungary, Serbia, Slovakia, and the Czech Republic. Transylvania, which means "Land Beyond the Forest," is an area in Romania that is frequently associated with vampires. According to a Romanian folktale, "There was a time when vampires were as common as leaves of grass, or berries in a pail, and they never kept still, but wandered round at night among the people."

It's not clear where the vampire folklore of eastern European stories got started. Some scholars think the stories evolved out of Greek and Roman mythology. Others believe that the Romany people (also called Gypsies) carried their stories into Europe when they migrated out of India around the thirteenth century.

During the Middle Ages, Christianity began to take hold in Europe. As the new religion butted heads with other religious beliefs, vampires became pawns in the battle. When the church got involved, vampires weren't just nasty creatures. They were worse. They were the work, and the workers, of Satan. The church spread the word that people who didn't believe in or disobeyed God were likely to end up as vampires.

In the early 1700s, vampires went public. A rash of vampire attacks in eastern Europe made the papers. These reports spread into western Europe and eventually became the basis of the modern image of vampires.

CHAPTER 3

DEALING WITH THE UNDEAD

VAMPIRES were bad news, but to people in the Middle Ages, they were often a fact of life. If you think you have it rough having to put up with your weird uncle, think of someone your age in medieval Europe. He might have to put up with his weird uncle, too—even after his uncle had returned from the dead.

AN OUNCE OF PREVENTION

There were several ways to become a vampire. Sometimes people were "infected" by another vampire when bitten. Sometimes the condition was inherited. Fate played a part, and so did a person's actions.

The risks started even before a person was born. Pregnant women had to be sure to eat enough salt and avoid eye contact with a vampire. Illegitimate children (those born to parents who weren't married) were in danger, as was the seventh child of the same sex. Infants born with a caul (a membrane around the head) were believed to be destined to become vampires.

A priest baptizes a baby. Baptism, a Christian ritual that symbolically washes away a person's sins, was considered one of the most basic measures needed to prevent someone from turning into a vampire.

If a person made it through all the dangers of pregnancy and infancy, he or she still had to stay vigilant in his or her lifestyle. Evil or sinful behavior could push someone right over the edge into vampirism.

Baptism was a must. A person couldn't have a brother who was a sleepwalker and couldn't eat sheep killed by a wolf. Because it was believed that vampires could change into other animals, including wolves, people thought that this meat could have been infected.

When it came time to die, a person couldn't do it by drowning. And he or she definitely couldn't commit suicide. In a somewhat unfair addition to this list, people who died violent deaths—such as by being murdered— were also at risk, even if they had done nothing wrong themselves.

Any involvement with the supernatural practically guaranteed admission into the After-Death Academy. You can just imagine parents sitting their children down for a stern lecture: "Now, it might seem like a good idea at the time, but don't become a werewolf! And above all, don't get mixed up with vampires!"

DEFENSIVE MEASURES

There were even more roadblocks after death. The living had a whole list of dos and don'ts as they took care of the corpse. For example, if an animal—especially a cat—jumped over a dead body, it put the person at risk to become a vampire. The corpse should not be touched by the wind, shadows, or moonlight.

A person who was "at risk" got special burial procedures. He should be buried facedown or at a crossroads. That way, he would be too confused to find his way back home. Better yet, make sure he can't get out of the

SILVER SOLUTIONS

Along with garlic and crucifixes, an excellent defense against vampires was silver. Silver was considered the "purest" of the metals, and purity was the ideal way to fend off evil. Ancient peoples used silver to disinfect food and water, and to treat wounds. Why not use it on vampires, too?

In mythology, silver is associated with the ancient Roman goddess Diana, who protected people. Vampires' hatred of silver might also have something to do with Christianity. Judas Iscariot was a disciple of Jesus Christ's. However, Judas betrayed Jesus and took a bribe of thirty pieces of silver. Although he later regretted his actions and tried to return the money, it was not accepted. Judas then hanged himself. Because he committed suicide, some think that Judas could have become a vampire—doomed to this fate over thirty pieces of silver.

grave in the first place. Tie up his feet, wrap his body in a cloth, and weigh it down with stones. Or, hammer it into the coffin with nails or stakes. Stuff his mouth with coins, garlic, or dirt, so he can't chew his way out of the grave.

Still feeling nervous? For added protection, cut off the head and bury it separately. That way, the vampire must find his head before he can go about his midnight mischief. If cutting off the head is too much to stomach, leave this grisly task to the vampire himself. By burying the body with a sickle positioned over its neck, people ensured that the vampire would cut off his own head if he tried to escape. Talk about grave consequences!

There were kinder, gentler approaches, too. For example, people sometimes buried food with the body to prevent it leaving the grave for a midnight snack. Candles were buried with people to light the soul's way into heaven—and not come back to pester the living.

Vampires had their flaws. For one thing, they seemed to be obsessed with order and organization. An easy way to distract a vampire was to sprinkle seeds or rice around the grave. When the vampire came out, he would get sidetracked by counting the seeds. The task might keep him busy until dawn, when he would be forced to turn in for the day. Another approach was to tie a corpse up using many little knots. The vampire would become so absorbed in untying the knots that he would neglect to get on with his blood-sucking business.

If a vampire still managed to get to your door, you

Misplaced your crucifix? No good at knots? Some methods of warding off vampires were dangerous or time-consuming, but one popular remedy—eating or wearing garlic—was easy, inexpensive, and available to almost anyone.

WEEKEND PLANS

Sabbatarians were people who were born on a Saturday. The Balkan people believed that these individuals had a special power to see vampires that were invisible to other people. Also, they believed that Saturdays were the ideal day to find and kill vampires because they were stuck in their coffins on Saturdays. In the Jewish religion, Saturday was the Sabbath (a day for God). In Christianity, at least part of the vampire's Saturday night fell on Sunday—the Christian Sabbath. Vampires did not want to be out and about at those times.

could cover it with tar so that he would get stuck or surround it with thorns to prick him.

On the eve of St. George's Day, when vampires were thought to be extremely active, people would ring the church bells, believing that they would keep vampires away. They also put garlic on the doors of their houses, turned out all the lights, and scattered the silverware for protection.

People used other objects to repel vampires, too, from candles to crucifixes, holly to holy water, and rice to roses. Some people even believed in a little reverse psychology. They ate food that contained blood to prevent vampire attacks.

SEEK AND DESTROY

Most people in the Middle Ages had typical jobs like farming or making goods. However, a few found a more unusual profession: vampire hunting. Armed with their tools of the trade, they would assist vampire-infested villages in ridding themselves of their nightly visitors. Certain people had the skills required for this job.

Dhampirs were believed to be part vampire: they were the sons of a male vampire and a human woman (often the vampire's widow). Dhampirs were kind of like vampire bloodhounds: because they had vampire blood, they were especially good at sniffing them out. They often acted out of revenge because they were angry at vampires for taking away their chance for a normal life. Killing a vampire brought its own satisfaction, but dhampirs were also well-paid for their services.

Vampires could change shape and disguise themselves as humans. They vanished each night. Before people could pin a vampire down with a wooden stake, they had to pin down his location and identify him clearly as a vampire.

Fingerprints and driver's licenses didn't help; fortunately, there were other tricks of the trade for the vampire detective. One method was to send a black horse through a cemetery. If the horse reached a grave and refused to cross over it, it was a sure sign that a vampire lived there. Another method was for a vampire hunter to fashion the sleeve of his shirt into a telescope, through which he could then see the vampire.

Vampires could also be tricked. For example, a vampire hunter might play music to coax a vampire into the open. Putting a little bit of blood in a bottle was a way to lure a vampire (who would change into mist or fog)

It's a dirty job, but somebody's got to do it. In this engraving from the sixteenth or seventeenth century, vampire slayers open a coffin and kill its inhabitant by stabbing its heart with a hot poker.

into the bottle. Then the hunter would shove a stopper into the bottle, trapping the vampire. People also believed that vampires were concerned about their clothes. Some hunters combined this weakness with another: water. The hunter could steal the vampire's clothes while he was asleep in his grave and then throw them into water. When the vampire tried to get them back, he drowned.

To kill a vampire, cutting off its head or piercing its heart with a wooden stake (or both) was standard procedure. It was important to do the job well. In Russia, driving the stake into the corpse needed to happen with a single blow. A second blow would actually bring the vampire back to "life."

Fire was another option. Burning a corpse robbed the vampire of the physical body he needed to travel. However, as the body burned, snakes, worms, maggots, and other vile creatures would pour from the body. It was important to make sure they burned, too. If even one got loose, the vampire could escape in it—alive (or at least still undead) and well.

THE MAKING OF A MYTH

MOST people today don't believe vampires exist. But if vampires aren't real, then where did all these vampire myths come from? Rituals and superstitions were important in older cultures. They gave a sense of order to a world that people didn't fully understand. Vampires helped explain the mysteries of death and disease and showed the consequences of not following the rules.

BREAK IT DOWN

When someone dies, his or her body decays. Several hundred years ago, some of the changes that occur during this process seemed strange to people. They thought these changes meant someone was becoming a vampire. Indeed, the physical description of a vampire closely matched that of a decaying corpse—in either case, it wasn't a pretty picture.

After death, gases build up in the body. They cause a corpse to become bloated and swollen, a condition that people sometimes mistook for a "well-fed"

vampire. Bacteria grow inside the corpse, and changes in the blood make the skin appear dark—just like a vampire. Organs may burst and blood may leak out of the corpse's mouth. Surely that was evidence that the vampire hadn't used a napkin after his nighttime feeding. The skin dries out, shrinks, and pulls back. This makes it look like the hair and fingernails have grown. But how could such a thing happen if the body was truly dead?

Gases being released from the body during decomposition isn't a quiet process either. It can produce the shrieks or groans that people assumed were the vampire's voice.

Premature burial was another problem. Death isn't always obvious. Occasionally, someone was believed to be dead when he or she was actually still alive. If the body was dug up later, people might see that it had moved. They interpreted

Victims of the plague were often buried in mass graves called plague pits. Medieval people did not understand how bacteria caused illness and often blamed vampires for spreading diseases.

IN THE BLOOD

Ancient cultures believed in the power of blood. The evidence was clear: people who lost a lot of blood usually died. It seemed logical that the reverse also was true: taking in blood could give a person energy and power. Vikings used to drink the blood of their enemies in order to become better warriors. The Romans drank the blood of gladiators to cure diseases. Sacrifices—killing people or animals and offering up their blood—was believed to be a way to please the gods. Some cultures thought that blood had its own soul. Taking another person's blood was a way to possess his soul.

this as a sign of vampirism, when it was actually evidence of a desperate attempt to escape. Today, most people are embalmed before being buried—a process that will kill them if they are not dead already—so being buried alive isn't too likely.

DISEASE

Vampires were also used to explain disease. In the fourteenth century, the bubonic plague raged through Europe, killing millions of people. People did not understand that it was bacteria that spread disease. Instead, they thought that death itself was on the loose. Some people believed that death was taken from person to person by vampires.

Just as with decomposing bodies, there was plenty of "evidence" to bolster this belief. In a form of the plague called pneumonic plague, a person's lungs are affected. He or she coughs up blood. So do people with tuberculosis, another lung disease. This blood around the mouth seemed like proof that vampires were at work.

Rabies is another horrible—and potentially fatal—disease. Victims would become violent and might try to bite. They would lose their senses and froth at the mouth. All of these symptoms matched those of a vampire attack.

Anemia is a blood disease in which people don't have enough red blood cells. They are often tired and look pale and sickly. These symptoms perfectly matched what would happen if vampires had fed on them.

Porphyria is a much rarer blood disease. The bodies of porphyria sufferers cannot make an ingredient in blood called heme. Their symptoms include extreme sensitivity to sunlight, which makes their skin blister, and a tightening of the skin, which makes their teeth more prominent. In 1985, a scientist named David Dolphin suggested that people with porphyria might be mistaken for vampires—and might even drink others' blood in an instinctive attempt to get the heme they needed. However, his theory was dismissed. It was based on the behavior of fictional vampires, not the ones of folklore.

MYTH MOTIVES

What people used to blame on vampires can now be explained through science. At the time, however, vampires provided an explanation. It was a

violent, scary, and often gross explanation, but it seemed rational. People didn't understand how bacteria could eat away at a body, so they looked for something they could understand: vampires.

In a strange way, vampires gave people power. The things people fear most are those that they can't control. By putting a face—even an ugly face with bad breath—to their fears, people gave themselves a little bit of control. If they thought that death and disease were caused by vampires, they could take steps to stop them. Of course, this wasn't easy. But it wasn't impossible. And that little bit of hope was better than none.

Vampires served another purpose. People rallied around the idea of vampires. Just as today we form our own mini-cults around *American Idol*, centuries ago, vampire stories brought people together and gave them something in common. For example, with their dark hair and eyes, the Greeks did not trust people

Vampires rested in their coffins while waiting for their chance to come out and feed. People believed that vampires' bodies did not decay normally because they sustained themselves on the living.

with blue eyes. They believed these people were susceptible to becoming vampires. Throw in some red hair and the chances were even better.

The Albanians did not trust their neighbors, the Turks. Albanians thought a person was likely to become a vampire if he had been born to Turkish parents, attended a Muslim religious service, or even ate meat that had been touched by a Turk.

Fear of strangers, fear of death, fear of the unknown: all of these could be assigned to vampires. Finally, vampires were like the bogeymen of medieval times. If you didn't behave, they would "get you!"

THE ROLE OF RELIGION

As Christianity moved into Europe, religion began to play a part in vampire mythology. The Greek Orthodox Church borrowed elements of these stories to promote the Christian religion. People who sinned were especially likely to become vampires. This was tied up in the idea of the body decomposing. A body that didn't decay was more attractive to a wandering soul. The church said that people had to be formally forgiven of their sins or else their bodies would not decompose, making them likely to become vampires.

If people committed especially terrible sins, they might be excommunicated. This meant that they were formally thrown out of the church. They would no longer receive the blessings of the church in life or its protection after death. Early Christians in Greece believed that, as part of the process of excommunication, clergy members could prevent a body from decaying after death. On the other hand, if these priests were feeling charitable, they could pardon sinful souls—even after they had died. In one instance, villagers dug up the body of a suspected vampire and placed a

written letter on the corpse forgiving him of past sins. These beliefs gave the church enormous power to influence people's behavior and ensure their faithfulness.

Interestingly, in the 1700s the Catholic Church argued against a belief in vampires, which put it in direct opposition to the Greek Orthodox Church and set the stage for a religious power struggle.

SCIENCE, THE VAMPIRE SLAYER

In 1725, a Serbian man named Peter Plogojowitz died. His relatives then reported that he returned as a vampire. However, his family wanted nothing to do with him after death. He then proceeded to kill people from his village. About the same time, another Serbian man named Arnold Paole also died and returned as a vampire. He, too, killed several people from his village. Seized with fear, the villagers dug up the bodies of these suspected vampires. Sure enough, the bodies were thought to show signs of vampire activity. The villagers promptly re-killed them by skewering the corpses with wooden stakes.

By the 1700s, western Europe was entering the Age of Reason. Science was making inroads into explaining the mysteries of life and death. The cases of Peter Plogojowitz and Arnold Paole, in eastern Europe, ran squarely up against the new scientific thinking. Many people still believed in the traditional mythology of vampires—that they existed, that they caused harm, and that they could be killed using tried-and-true methods. Eastern Europeans may have clung to myths like these as a way to resist the fact that western Europe was making so much progress in learning and knowledge. A French monk named Antoine Augustin Calmet investigated these and other vampire incidents. In 1746, he published a paper attempting

R.P.Dom. AUGUSTINUS CALMET.
Monachus Congregat: SS. Vitoni & Hydulphi,
Prior de Layo.

French monk Antoine Augustin Calmet became a best-selling author in the 1700s, when he published a report about vampire activities. Many scholars didn't believe in vampires, but Calmet didn't seem entirely convinced.

to use science to explain what had happened. He also noted that the reports came mostly from "ignorant" peasants. However, he stopped short of saying that vampires did not exist. Other thinkers of the time were not so cautious. The outspoken French thinker Voltaire scoffed at the belief in vampires. The Catholic Church also denied their existence. Still, Calmet's treatise became a bestseller, introducing more people to the idea of vampires.

Vampire reports continued to come in over the next several years. In 1755, the empress of Austria, Maria Theresa, stepped in. She sent her personal doctor to look into supposed vampire activity. He reported back that vampires did not exist, and the empress promptly ordered a stop to opening graves and mutilating bodies of people who were already dead.

Science, at least for the moment, had won against the mythologies that people had believed in for centuries.

TRAITÉ
SUR LES
APPARITIONS
DES ESPRITS,
ET
SUR LES VAMPIRES,
OU LES REVENANS
de Hongrie, de Moravie, &c.

Par le R. P. Dom AUGUSTIN CALMET, Abbé de Sénones.

Nouvelle édition revûe, corrigée & augmentée par l'Auteur.

TOME I.

A PARIS,
Chez DEBURE l'aîné, Quai des Augustins, à l'Image S. Paul.

M. D. CC. LI.
Avec Approbation & Privilege du Roi.

Calmet's treatise on vampires helped popularize the idea of vampires. After it was published, more vampire incidents were reported throughout Europe.

CHAPTER
5

VAMPIRES IN MODERN TIMES

SCIENCE offered explanations for sickness, death, and even after-death. But what it couldn't do was satisfy people's appetite for mystery and danger. Although the controversy over "real" vampires died down in the second half of the eighteenth century, these creatures continued to live on in fiction.

FROM FOLKLORE TO FICTION

People were reluctant to give up their vampires entirely, so they found new jobs for them. One of these was entertainment. Vampires may feed on blood, but people feed on thrills, and few things give more of a thrill than an immortal bloodsucker. Vampires were still dangerous, but they were charming, too.

Several vampire stories were written in the nineteenth century. The most important was one that people still know of today: Bram Stoker's *Dracula*. Stoker based his vampire character on an actual person, a Romanian ruler in the 1400s named Vlad Dracula.

Vlad Dracula was called Vlad the Impaler because of how he liked to kill his enemies. Although he was not a vampire, his brutal behavior helped inspire Bram Stoker's fictional Dracula character.

He was also called Vlad Tepes. The word "Tepes" means "impaler." Vlad Tepes was a cruel warrior who sometimes killed his enemies by impaling them on stakes. He might have even drunk their blood! However, he was not a vampire.

Stoker's *Dracula* was first published in 1897. Many movies were later based on this classic tale. The fictional Dracula became the yardstick by which all other vampires were measured. Unlike the vampires of folklore, Dracula had an elegant streak. Granted, he had fangs, bad breath, and the annoying habit of changing into a bat. But compared to some of the figures that crept out of the local cemetery, he was more than tolerable.

In the late twentieth century, vampires became even more popular. Author Anne Rice published *Interview with the Vampire* in the 1970s. Her main vampire, Lestat, was likable. *Buffy the Vampire Slayer* was a movie and later a television show that told vampire stories from the point of view of the hunter—a spunky high school girl. Today, Stephenie Meyer's *Twilight* books feature an entire family of vampires. The books' main character, Bella, becomes romantically involved with one of the vampires. They also face trouble from rival vampires.

MONSTER MAKEOVER

Unlike the vampires of several centuries ago, the vampires in modern fiction are not disgusting creatures. Instead, they're often attractive and likable. Their lives, while certainly unusual, aren't necessarily awful. And even if their actions are disgusting, the characters themselves are often sympathetic. Their thirst for blood is not so much a tragic fate than it is a pesky character flaw.

DO THE MATH

A physics professor from Florida claimed in 2005 that vampires couldn't exist because it was statistically impossible. Basing his theory on the belief that vampires are created by other vampires, he made a chart that showed how vampires would soon outnumber humans. If, starting in 1600, a vampire bit one person a month, it would take only two and a half years for all the humans to have been turned into vampires, leaving them no food source!

As they've evolved, vampires have acquired some more powers, too. They're often super-strong and fast, making it easy for them to overpower their victims. Their senses—such as sight and hearing—are much stronger than an ordinary human's. They can fly and climb up sheer walls. They don't cast shadows, can't be photographed, and aren't reflected in mirrors. And of course, they hate sunlight. All of these are relatively modern vampire traits. They were invented by the authors of fictional vampires and adopted into the general folklore. Earlier vampires had no problem with sunlight and were often quite vain, fascinated with examining their own reflections in mirrors.

Dracula was published in the late 1800s. This was known as the Victorian Era, after England's Queen Victoria. During this time, people—especially women—were expected to be extremely reserved and proper in public. Vampire stories, however, gave them a forbidden pleasure. Associating with the undead was clearly not behavior that would be accepted in society. However, if it was just a story, then it was all right—it was all in fun.

By the twentieth century, social norms were changing again. People had more freedom in how to express themselves. However, it didn't mean that everyone was accepted by everyone else.

Author Anne Rice has said that her vampires were a "metaphor for the outsider." Many people have felt shut out or disconnected at some time or another, and a vampire represents this.

In Stephenie Meyer's blockbuster Twilight series, high school student Bella Swan thinks she's found her soul mate in Edward Cullen, a mysterious boy who turns out to be a vampire and complicates Bella's life.

He looks odd, has strange nighttime habits, and doesn't eat normal food. And you thought you were weird? Nothing like a vampire to put you right back in the mainstream!

THE TRADITION LIVES ON

Most people didn't believe in real vampires by the end of the twentieth century, but some did. In 2004, in a village in Romania, a man named Toma Petre was suspected of being a vampire. His relatives dug up his body and burned his heart. Then, according to tradition, they mixed the ashes with water and drank them. The police accused the man's relatives of "disturbing the peace of the dead," which was a crime.

Toma Petre's relatives did not believe they had done anything wrong. According to them, they were simply stopping the vampire from killing people from beyond the grave. The offenders received a prison sentence, but it was later reduced. This was partly because an expert in Romanian folk traditions explained that the people had not deliberately committed a crime. Instead, they had only acted according to their longstanding beliefs.

The case of Toma Petre wasn't the only one. More stories came out that other Romanians had done similar things. Gheorghe Sandu, the police commissioner for Toma Petre's village, said: "I'd like to be able to say this village is unique, but unfortunately I can't because I know just how strong belief in vampires is here."

A few years later, in 2007, a man visited the grave of Slobodan Milosevic, who had been the president of Yugoslavia. Milosevic was called the Butcher of the Balkans. He was accused of helping to kill thousands of people during wartime. The man who came to Milosevic's grave drove a

Mourners visit the grave of Yugoslavian president Slobodan Milosevic. One year after his death, another man drove a stake into the grave to prevent Milosevic, who was a brutal leader, from becoming a vampire.

stake through the grave exactly one year after Milosevic's death, in order to prevent him from becoming a vampire.

A NEW MYTHOLOGY

If vampires were awful, fearful creatures for so many centuries, why do people today like them so much? For one thing, the fear of a vampire actually showing up in your kitchen or cornfield has gone.

VAMPIRES FOR KIDS

Vampires have become such an accepted part of our culture that some of them have gotten positively cuddly. On the children's television show *Sesame Street*, it's a vampire who teaches children how to count. Count Chocula is a vampire who helps sell breakfast cereal.

In the 1970s, a children's book called *Bunnicula* featured a vampire pet bunny. Bunnicula wasn't dangerous, though—he only sucked the vegetables dry. The vegetarian vampire was born. A British television show called *Count Duckula* aired in the 1980s and 1990s. This vampire duck used to survive the traditional way—by sucking blood. However, one time there was mix-up, and the duck got ketchup instead of blood. These stories were used as ways to teach children tolerance of people (or animals) who were different.

On the other hand, the advantages of being a vampire remain. They're immortal (as long as they can avoid people wielding wooden stakes). They have amazing strength and a long list of interesting abilities. Vampires also represent the dark side of human beings. From time to time, everyone wants to do things they know they shouldn't. Vampires can offer a kind of "excuse" to enjoy bad behavior.

They survive, and even thrive, even though they are different from everybody else. In a world where there are so many things beyond our control, it can be fun to identify with a creature who can escape it all. We came to love vampires in spite of—and eventually because of—what they are.

In her book *Our Vampires, Ourselves*, Nina Auerbach wrote that successful vampires know how to change with the times. Their look, their abilities, their appeal—everything about them perfectly fits their society and culture. "[Vampires] can be everything we are, while at the same time, they are fearful reminders of the infinite things we are not," she wrote.

Vampires have survived for thousands of years. At times they have sucked us dry. But in a way they've also fed us, giving us a way to explain our world and find our place in it. The stories we tell and the things we believe are always changing, but vampires, in some form or another, will probably always be a part of it. It may be possible to kill a vampire, but not even a stake through the heart will kill their role in mythology.

TIMELINE

PREHISTORY

Vampire-like creatures appear in myths from cultures all over the world.

1047

The word *upir* (later to become "vampire") first appears in written form.

1100s

English scholars record written accounts of reported vampire activity.

1200s

The Romany people (Gypsies) begin migrating from India into Europe.

1300s

Some people blame vampires for the bubonic plague outbreak in Europe.

1428

Romanian ruler Vlad Tepes is born; he is later used as the basis for the fictional character of Count Dracula.

1700s

Vampire hysteria erupts in Europe.

1725–1726

Serbian men Arnold Paole and Peter Plogojowitz are suspected of being vampires.

1746

Dom Augustin Calmet publishes his treatise on vampires.

1755

Austrian empress Maria Theresa outlaws grave mutilations after her investigator concludes that vampires do not exist.

1800s

Vampires begin to appear in works of fiction.

1897

Bram Stoker's *Dracula* is published.

1928

Historian Montague Summers publishes *The Vampire: His Kith and Kin*, a collection of vampire folklore.

1976

Anne Rice's *Interview with a Vampire* is published.

1985

Scientist David Dolphin proposes a link between vampirism and a blood disease called porphyria. His theory is later dismissed.

2004

The relatives of a deceased Romanian man burn the body and consume its ashes to prevent the corpse from becoming a vampire.

2005

Author Stephenie Meyer publishes the first book in her Twilight series.

2007

A man drives a stake through the heart of deceased Yugoslavian president Slobodan Milosevic, saying it was to prevent Milosevic from becoming a vampire.

2008

Archaeologists discover a grave from the Bronze Age in which the body was weighted down with stones. They believe this was done to prevent the body from leaving the grave.

archaeologist A scholar who studies bones and other physical remains of people or animals.

consequences Results that happen because of a certain action.

decompose To decay; break down.

disheveled Messy; unkempt.

embalm To preserve a dead body by injecting it with certain chemicals.

grisly Gruesome; horrible.

immortal Able to live forever; unable to be killed.

impale To stab something through with a sharp object, such as a stake.

metaphor A description or example used to represent or illustrate something similar.

mythology Stories and beliefs used to explain events in a culture.

perks Advantages or benefits to a certain situation.

prominent Something that stands out from the things around it; more obvious or important.

prototype The first example of something.

re-animated To have lifelike abilities restored.

reluctant Hesitant; unwilling.

revenant Something that has returned from the dead.

sacrifice An offering made to a god.

sickle A type of tool used for cutting.

susceptible Vulnerable; likely to be affected by something.

sustenance Something needed to stay alive, such as food.

territorial To be protective of a certain territory or area.

vigilant Determined; committed.

Dracula Society

P.O. Box 30848

London W12 0GY

United Kingdom

Web site: http://www.thedraculasociety.org.uk

Formed in 1973, the Dracula Society hosts meetings, events, and travel opportunities for people interested in vampires.

Romanian National Tourist Office

355 Lexington Avenue, 8th Floor

New York, NY 10017

(212) 545-8484

E-mail: info@romaniatourism.com

Web site: http://www.romaniatourism.com

The Romanian National Tourist Office has information relating to Romania's cultural history of vampires.

Spellbound Museum

192 Essex Street

Salem, MA

(978) 744-1463

Web site: http://www.spellboundtours.com/spellbound_museum.htm

The Spellbound Museum offers tours that include local vampire lore and maintains a small museum with vampire artifacts.

T.A.P.S.

2363 West Shore Road

Warwick, RI 02889

E-mail: help@the-atlantic-paranormal-society.com

Web site: http://the-atlantic-paranormal-society.com

Teams with the Atlantic Paranormal Society investigate claims of paranormal activity all over the United States.

Transylvanian Society of Dracula

Postfach 250411

50520 Koln (Cologne)

Germany

Phone: 49-173-287-3136

E-mail: tsd@benecke.com

Web site: http://www.benecke.com

The president of the German chapter of the Transylvanian Society of Dracula is a forensic researcher and expert in vampirism.

University of Victoria

Department of Germanic and Slavic Studies

Clearihue Building, Room D243

P.O. Box 3045

Victoria, BC V8W 3P4

Canada

(250) 721-7316

E-mail: geru@uvic.ca

Web site: http://web.uvic.ca/geru/index.html

German and Slavic cultures, including the role of vampires, are studied in this department at the University of Victoria, whose faculty includes a leading vampire scholar.

University of Virginia

Department of Slavic Languages and Literature

P.O. Box 400783

Charlottesville, VA 22904-4783

(434) 924-3548

Web site: http://artsandsciences.virginia.edu/slavic

The Slavic Languages and Literature Department of the University of Virginia studies Slavic cultures and offers insight into vampire myths that originated in the region.

WEB SITES

Due to the changing nature of Internet links, Rosen Publishing has developed an online list of Web sites related to the subject of this book. This site is updated regularly. Please use this link to access the list:

http://www.rosenlinks.com/vamp/vim

FOR FURTHER READING

Allman, Toney. *Werewolves*. Farmington Hills, MI: KidHaven Press, 2009.

Besel, Jennifer M. *Vampires*. Mankato, MN: Capstone, 2006.

Brewer, Heather. *Eighth Grade Bites*. New York, NY: Speak, 2008.

Cary, Kate. *Bloodline*. New York, NY: Razorbill, 2006.

Cybulski, Angela. *Vampires: Fact or Fiction?* Farmington Hills, MI:
    Greenhaven Press, 2003.

DK Publishing. *The Vampire Book*. New York, NY: 2009.

Gee, Joshua. *Encyclopedia Horrifica: The Terrifying Truth! About Vampires,
    Ghosts, Monsters and More*. New York, NY: Scholastic, 2007.

Goldberg, Enid A. *Vlad the Impaler: The Real Count Dracula*. New York,
    NY: Franklin Watts, 2007.

Guiley, Rosemary Ellen. *Vampires*. New York, NY: Checkmark Books, 2009.

Hamby, Zachary. *Mythology for Teens: Classic Myths for Today's World*.
    Austin, TX: Prufrock Press, 2009.

Hamilton, John. *Vampires*. Edina, MN: ABDO Publishing, 2007.

Hautman, Pete. *Sweetblood*. New York, NY: Simon Pulse, 2004.

Hofer, Charles. *Meet Dracula*, New York, NY: Rosen Publishing, 2005.

Jinks, Catherine. *The Reformed Vampire Support Group*. New York, NY:
    Harcourt Children's Books, 2009.

Kallen, Stuart. *Vampires*. San Diego, CA: ReferencePoint Press, 2008.

Krensky, Stephen. *Vampires*. Minneapolis, MN: Lerner Publications
    Company, 2007.

Martin, Dawn. *Vampires*. Duncan, SC: Hammond Undercover, 2009.

McMeans, Bonnie. *Vampires*. Farmington Hills, MI: KidHaven Press, 2006.

Meyer, Stephenie. *Twilight*. New York, NY: Little, Brown Books for Young
    Readers, 2005.

Miller, Raymond. *Vampires*. Farmington Hills, MI: KidHaven Press, 2005.

Pratchett, Terry. *Carpe Jugulum*. New York, NY: HarperTorch, 2000.

Rook, Sebastian. *The Vampire Plagues: London, 1850*. New York, NY: Scholastic, 2005.

Shan, Darren. *Cirque du Freak*. New York, NY: Little, Brown Books for Young Readers, 2002.

Sloan, Christopher. *Bury the Dead: Tombs, Corpses, Mummies, Skeletons, and Rituals*. Washington, DC: National Geographic Society, 2002.

Stefoff, Rebecca. *Vampires, Zombies and Shape-Shifters*. Tarrytown, NY: Marshall Cavendish Benchmark, 2008.

Taylor, Joules. *Vampires*. London, England: Spruce, 2009.

Wallace, Anne Sharp. *The Gypsies*. Farmington Hills, MI: Lucent Books, 2002.

BIBLIOGRAPHY

Auerbach, Nina. *Our Vampires, Ourselves*. Chicago, IL: University of Chicago Press, 1995.

Barber, Paul. *Vampires, Burial, and Death: Folklore and Reality*. New Haven, CT: Yale University Press, 1988.

Bartlett, Wayne, and Flavia Idriceanu. *Legends of Blood: The Vampire in History and Myth*. Westport, CT: Praeger Publishers, 2006.

Beresford, Matthew. *From Demons to Dracula: The Creation of the Modern Vampire Myth*. London, England: Reaktion Books, 2008.

Bernheisel, Steve. "In the Blood: A Serious Look at Vampire-Myth Origins." Lesvampires.org. Retrieved December 10, 2009 (http://www.lesvampires.org/mirrorsportal/bernheisel.html).

Curran, Bob. *Vampires: A Field Guide to the Creatures That Stalk the Night*. Franklin Lakes, NJ: The Career Press, Inc., 2005.

Day, William Patrick. *Vampire Legends in Contemporary American Culture: What Becomes a Legend Most*. Lexington, KY: University Press of Kentucky, 2002.

Frost, Brian J. *The Monster with a Thousand Faces: Guises of the Vampire in Myth and Literature*. Bowling Green, OH: Bowling Green State University Popular Press, 1989.

Gordon, Joan, and Veronica Hollinger. *Blood Read: The Vampire as Metaphor in Contemporary Culture*. Philadelphia, PA: University of Pennsylvania Press, 1997.

Hallab, Mary Y. *Vampire God: The Allure of the Undead in Western Culture*. Albany, NY: State University of New York Press, 2009.

Mascetti, Manuela Dunn. *Vampire: The Complete Guide to the World of the Undead*. New York, NY: Viking Studio Books, 1992.

McClelland, Bruce. *Slayers and Their Vampires: A Cultural History of Killing the Dead*. Ann Arbor, MI: University of Michigan Press, 2006.

McGrath, Adrian Nicholas. "Vampires: Origins of the Myth." Parascope. com. Retrieved December 18, 2009 (http://web.archive.org/web/19990203080329/parascope.com/en/articles/vampires.htm).

Melton, J. Gordon. *The Vampire Book: The Encyclopedia of the Undead*. Canton, MI: Visible Ink Press, 1999.

Monstrous.com. "Monstrous Vampires." Retrieved November 17, 2009 (http://vampires.monstrous.com/index.htm).

Perkowski, Jan L. *Vampire Lore: From the Writings of Jan Louis Perkowski*. Bloomington, IN: Slavica Publishers, 2006.

Ramsland, Katherine M. *The Science of Vampires*. New York, NY: Berkley Publishing Group, 2002.

Stevenson, Jay. *The Complete Idiot's Guide to Vampires*. Indianapolis, IN: Alpha Books, 2002.

Summers, Montague. *The Vampire in Lore and Legend*. Mineola, NY: Dover Publications, 2001.

Thorne, Tony. *Children of the Night: Of Vampires and Vampirism*. London, England: Indigo, 2000.

Wright, Dudley. *Vampires and Vampirism: Legends from Around the World*. Maple Shade, NJ: Lethe Press, 2001.

INDEX

ABOUT THE AUTHOR

Diane Bailey has written several books for children and teens, on topics ranging from celebrities to sports. She particularly enjoys exploring history and delving into all the stories that go into creating cultures. She lives in Kansas with her two sons, two dogs—and no vampires.

PHOTO CREDITS

Cover © www.istockphotocom/David Pedre; p. 7 APIC/Getty Images; p. 9 V&A Images, London/Art Resource, NY; p. 11 Silver Screen Collection/Hulton Archive/Getty Images; pp. 15, 20 © AP Images; p. 17 SSPL/Getty Images; p. 23 Rob Melnychuk/Digital Vision/Getty Images; p. 26 Maxine Adcock/GAP Photos/Getty Images; pp. 29, 40 © Mary Evans Picture Library/The Image Works; pp. 32–33 http://ihm. nlm.nih.gov; pp. 36–37 © Topham/The Image Works; p. 41 © Lordprice Collection/Alamy; p. 43 Simon Marsden/The Bridgeman Art Library/ Getty Images; pp. 46–47 © Maverick Films/Zuma Press; p. 49 Dimitar Dilkoff/AFP/Getty Images; interior graphics (bats) adapted from Shutterstock.com.

Designer: Les Kanturek; Editor: Bethany Bryan;
Photo Researcher: Amy Feinberg